FLYING SQUIRRELS

FLYING
SQUIRRELS

MARY ANN MCDONALD

THE CHILD'S WORLD

561590

What was that shadow that passed under the stars? Did you see something fly between the trees? Now you hear a bird chirping—but it's dark outside and birds should be sleeping! If you live in a wooded area, you may have seen or heard a flying squirrel.

Flying squirrels are furry little rodents with big eyes. They are related to animals like the chipmunk, beaver, mouse, and squirrel. Their scientific name, *Glaucomys volans*, means "flying mouse." A full-grown flying squirrel is only five inches long, or about the size of a chipmunk. Its flat, furry tail is almost as long as its body!

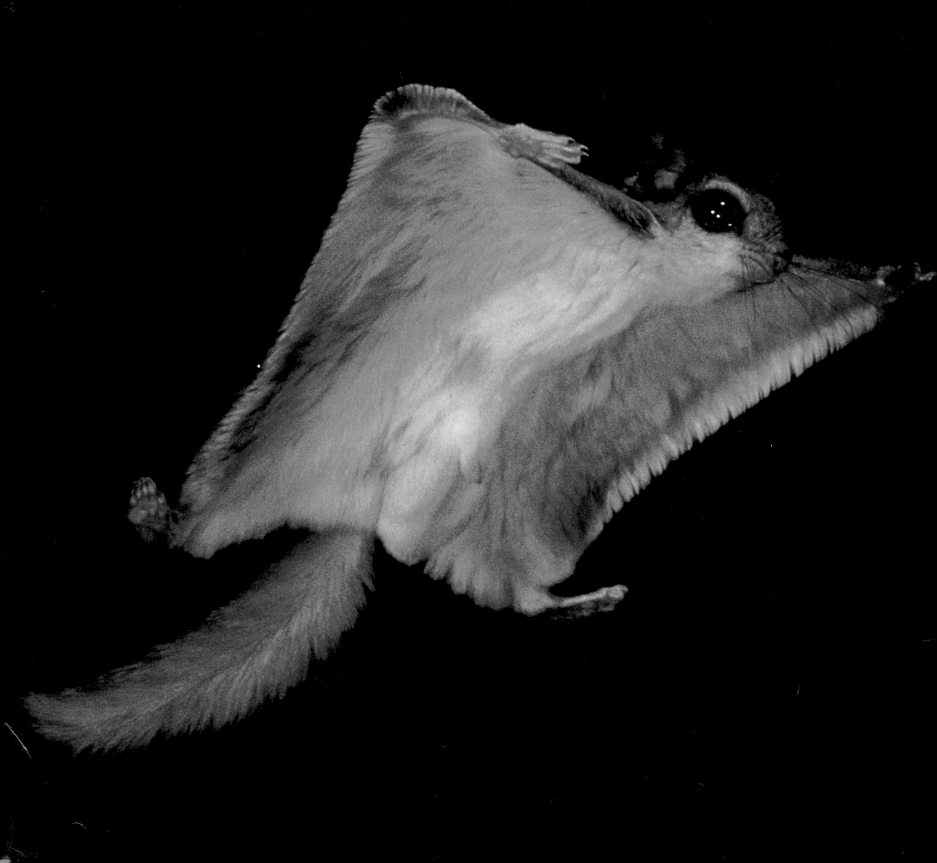

Flying squirrels don't really fly. They actually glide from one tree to another. Flying squirrels have a thin flap of skin called a *patagium* that stretches from their ankles to their wrists. To glide, a flying squirrel first climbs a tall tree. Then it jumps into the air and spreads its patagium, gliding downward to another tree. The squirrel's flat tail helps it steer as it sails through the air. A flying squirrel can glide as far as ninety yards. That's almost as long as a football field!

Flying squirrels don't always glide. Sometimes they simply jump from tree to tree without spreading their patagium. They can easily leap four feet. If you could jump like a flying squirrel, you would be able to jump across a two-lane street! On the ground, flying squirrels move about in short hops as they look for food.

Like their close relatives, red and gray squirrels, flying squirrels eat wild nuts. Their favorites are beechnuts, hickory nuts, and acorns. They eat other things, too, including tree buds and blossoms, berries, maple sap, and mushrooms. Sometimes they even eat insects, eggs, baby birds, and small mice!

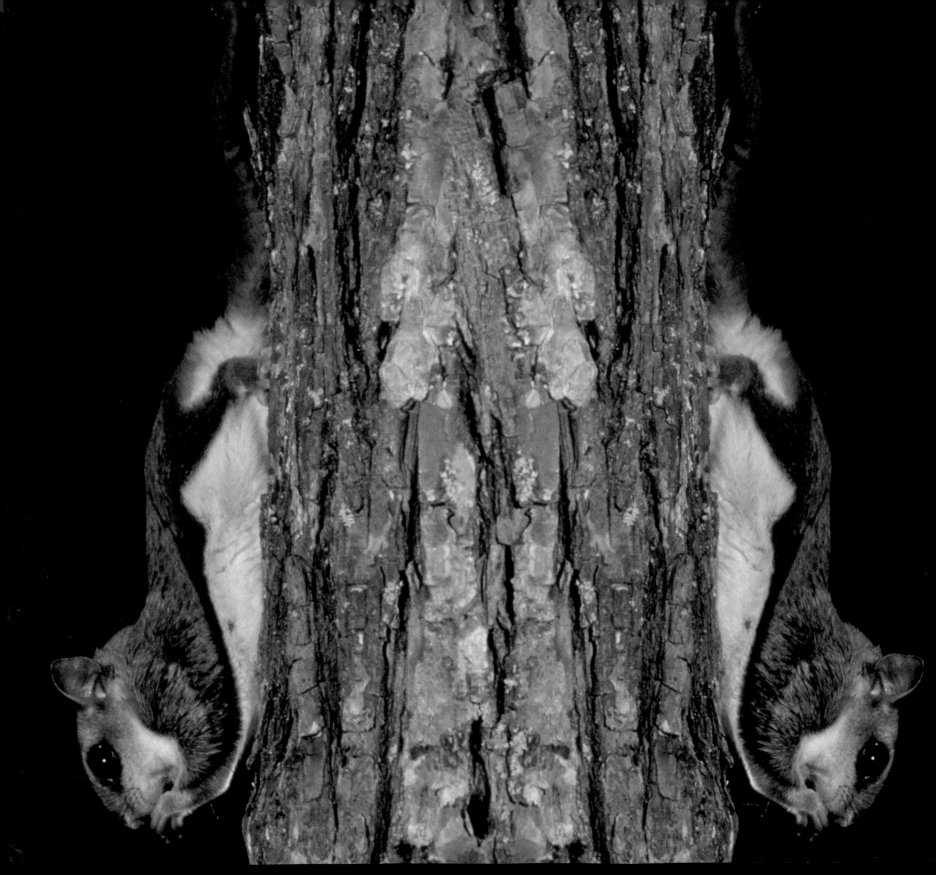

Flying squirrels sometimes hang upside down while they eat. They have sharp, curved claws that help them cling to trees. With their sharp claws, they can even land upside down on a tree!

Flying squirrels live mainly in forests of the eastern United States and Canada. But even if you live in these areas, you probably will never see a flying squirrel. Flying squirrels are *nocturnal*, which means they are active only at night. Their big black eyes help them see in the dark. They can see at night as well as you can during the day!

Flying squirrels have big ears that let them hear very well. They communicate with many sounds. They make a"chuck-chuck" sound when surprised or pleased. They squeak when they are upset and chirp like birds when playing. They use both their eyes and their ears to watch and listen for danger.

Flying squirrels have many enemies that they must watch out for—even at night. Barred and great horned owls are their worst enemies. Goshawks and red-tailed hawks also hunt flying squirrels. On the ground, the squirrels must avoid foxes, cats, and even rattlesnakes. Flying squirrels aren't safe during the day, either. Weasels, raccoons, and black rat snakes look for the squirrels in their nests.

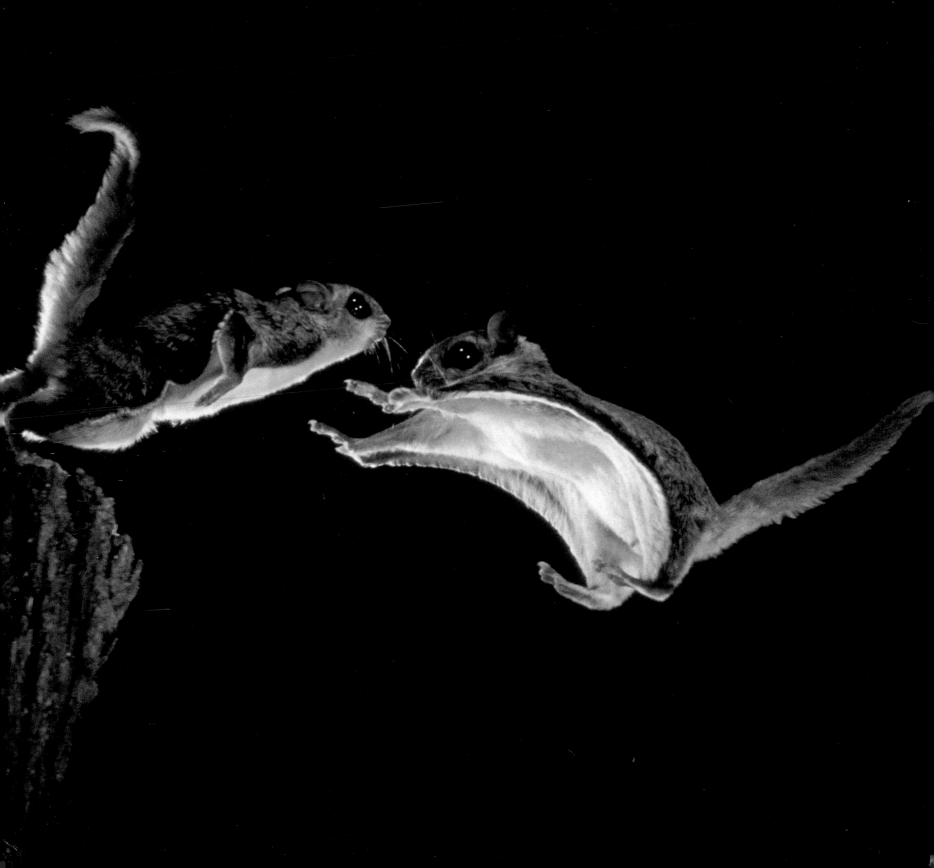

Flying squirrels have babies twice a year. Each litter has an average of four babies. Newborn flying squirrels are pink and hairless, and their eyes and ears are closed. After four weeks, the babies are covered with fur and their eyes and ears are open. Young squirrels drink their mother's milk. By seven weeks, they are looking for their own food and can make short glides. Young squirrels stay with their family through their first winter.

Flying squirrels don't hibernate during the winter. Instead, they remain active and look for food. If the temperature gets really cold, the squirrels snuggle together in their nests. These winter huddles provide protection and warmth for all the squirrels.

Flying squirrels are not afraid of humans. If you have a birdfeeder you can try feeding the squirrels. When it is almost dark, put a mixture of peanut butter and pecans in the feeder. It might take a couple of days for the squirrels to find your food, but if they live nearby, they will find it. Then get ready to have some fun! Once the squirrels come to the feeder, you can watch them with a flashlight as they "fly" among the trees.

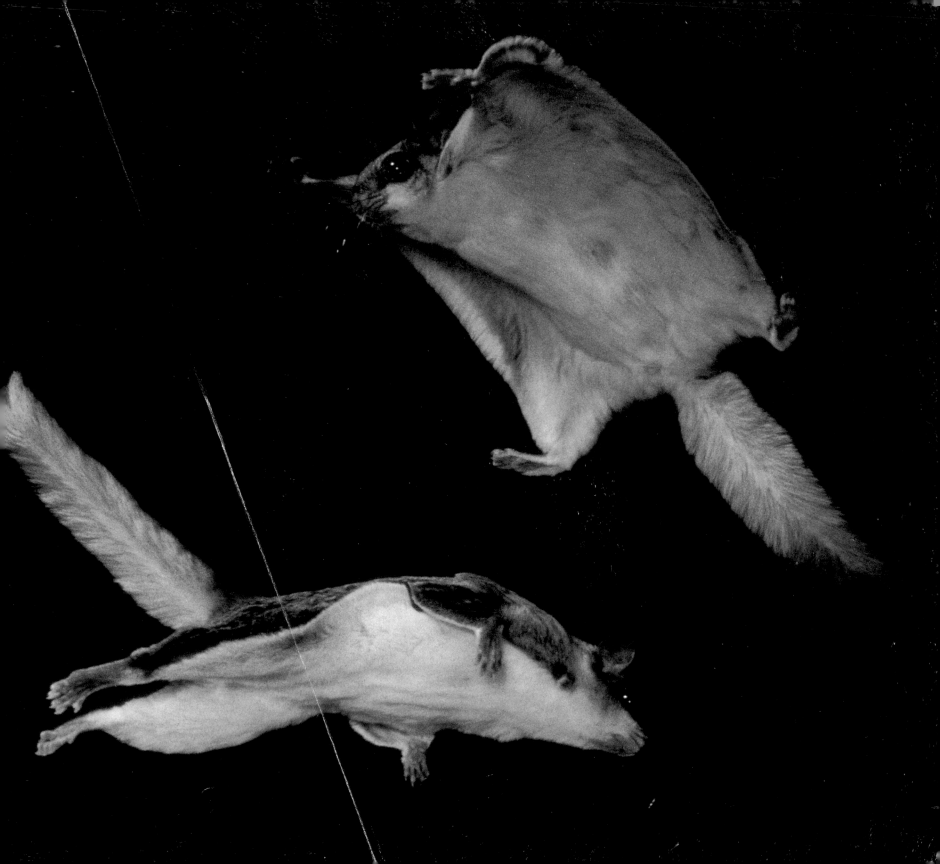

INDEX

babies, 27

claws, 15, 32

communication, 19

ears, 19, 27

eating, 12, 15

enemies, 20

eyes, 6, 16, 19, 27

flying, 9

food, 10, 24, 27, 29, 30

fur, 27

Glaucomys volans, 6

gliding, 9, 10

hanging, 15

hibernation, 29

jumping, 10

nests, 20, 23, 24, 29

patagium, 9, 10

range, 16

relatives, 6, 12

sight, 5, 16

size, 6, 32

tail, 6, 9

watching, 30

winter, 23, 27, 29

young, 27

PHOTO RESEARCH

Charles Rotter/Archipelago Productions

Photographs by Joe McDonald

Library of Congress Cataloging-in-Publication Data
McDonald, Mary Ann.
Flying squirrels / by Mary Ann McDonald.
p. cm.
Summary: Describes the physical characteristics,
habits, and life cycle of the nocturnal flying squirrel.
ISBN 1-56766-058-4
1. Flying squirrels--Juvenile literature.
[1. Flying squirrels.   2. Squirrels.]   I. Title.
QL737.R68M38   1993   93-9118
599.32'32--dc20

Distributed to schools and libraries in the United States by
ENCYCLOPAEDIA BRITANNICA EDUCATIONAL CORP.
310 South Michigan Avenue
Chicago, Illinois 60604